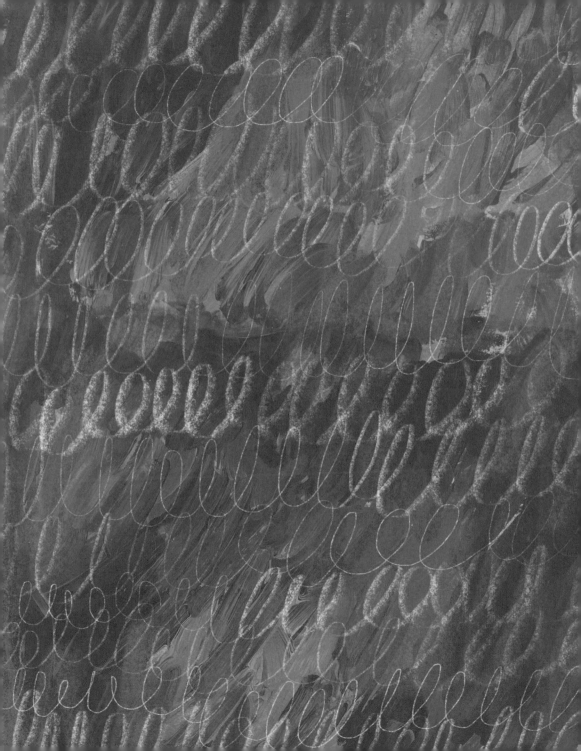

(I thought you could use a little surprise.)

The feeling you
got when you
opened it up?

That feeling's
from me.

(It's a whole lot of love.)

And I used all
the best hug
technology too...

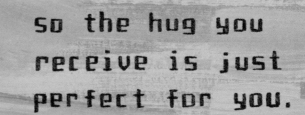

so the hug you
receive is just
perfect for you.

It's A Bear Hug
on Days when the
thing
you Most
need

is a Hug tHAt is ALmost entireLy squeeze

It's a side hug along with a stroll in the park while we look at the ducks and we chat until dark.

IT'S A HUG WITH HOT COCOA, A HUG WITH SOME PIE, IN A RESTAURANT BOOTH, WATCHING THE WORLD GO BY.

It's a hug that is
long But not
awkward at all.

It's a hug that comes through with a telephone call.

It's a hug that just makes you feel deeply at home

and at
ease in
the world,

and a
Bit less
alone.

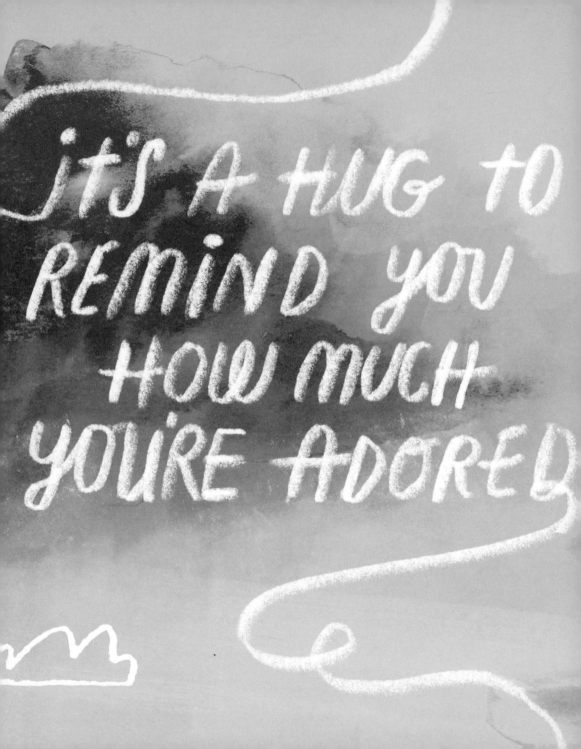

It's A Hug tHAt turns into

A couple Hugs more.

It's a hug
that can travel at
lightning speed.

It's a hug
that can span any
distance you need.

It's a hug that arrives
at the opportune time,
and the minute you feel it,
you'll know that it's mine.

And if there's a hug
that you think that
I've missed, you can
ask for it now,
and that hug will exist.

This isn't a book,

It will never wear out

Because if there's one thing

it's that no one deserves

it's a hug in disguise.

*

(but please feel free to try).

that I know to be true,

the BEST hugs more than you.

* PRESS TO YOUR HEART

COMPENDIUM.
live inspired

Written by: M.H. Clark
Illustrated by: Katie Vernon
Edited by: Amelia Riedler
Art Directed by: Megan Gandt

ISBN: 978-1-957891-10-1

*Create
meaningful
moments
with gifts
that inspire.*

CONNECT WITH US
live-inspired.com | sayhello@compendiuminc.com

@compendiumliveinspired
#compendiumliveinspired